THIS UNBEGOTTEN PARADISE

THIS UNBEGOTTEN PARADISE

By

WILLIAM M. BARRETT

ILLUSTRATED BY LEONARD GUARDINO

BOSTON
BRANDEN PRESS
PUBLISHERS

Standard Book Number 8283-1032-7

© Copyright, 1969, by Branden Press, Inc.
Printed in the United States of America
Library of Congress Catalog Card Number 70-80881

CONTENTS

This unbegotten paradise	9
Again For Bobby	10
A pocket full of sadness	12
Autopsy	13
Monastery on a hill	14
The two-legged child	16
Mon Ami	17
Codicil for a wayward poet	18
The inner ring	21
Words	22
The well of loneliness	24
Poetry night	25
Breathe easy, boy	26
Wherein the leopard eats his skin	27
Mi-lady	28
Into the night	29
Vespers at high noon	30
How to catch a metaphor	31
Cry the innocents abroad	32
An open letter to Yevtushenko	33
Prophesy	34
Next stop—heaven	35
Let joy be unconcerned	36
Somewhere	37
Johnny Appleseed	38
Fishing expedition	40
Hart Crane	42
Vengeance is mine	43
Only the wind remembers	44
Wiggly (The wench from Piggly Street)	45
Then I was merely a boy	47

The kiss is on the rose	48
And the world spins on	49
Why should I weep?	50
The bouquet woman	51
Oddly he dies	52
Maniac depressive	53
The whiskey rebellion	54
It's a long road	55
Wanted—A Minister of the Interior	56
All the world's a stage	57
Time is a dragon	58
During the night	59
Corridor of dreams	61
Lecture from my hospital bed	63
Menchen—menchen	64
Angels paradise	65
With both my hands	66
New wine for old	67
Man—supergod	68
Manhattan skyline	69
Farewell to farms	70
"Wherein doth lie the dread and fear of kings"	71
Old Bowery	72
Morning stroll	73
Save my child	74
Convocation	75
Descent and distribution	76
The Assyrians came down	77
The crowning	78
Will of the wisp	79
Consequently I'm it	80
How tall	82
Mamie at the hangin'	83
Unbend	85
Like bundles of snow	86
The bookends	87

Numbskull and gnat	88
The trespasser	89
Forever eighteen	90
Like Gaul	92
The island of my dreams	93
International harvester	94
When I was very young indeed	95
We counted seven	97
A poet is entitled to a nightmare	99
The harvest	100
Bitter plums	101

This unbegotten paradise

This skimpy little earth,
this accident of Nature,
or handiwork of God—
(if so you wish it)
stands all alone in this Creation's scheme of things.
Man putters with the Universe—
measures it for size,
temperature
air and water—
and finds it quite unblessed,
unfruitful, uninhabited—
dead.
The brightest star which flickers in the firmament
is a drab, stony, lifeless desert:
and man makes poetry out of nothing,
out of rolling globs of stone rushing in a senseless orbit
around a larger glob of molten stone.
The happy zealots fill the skies with gods and goddesses,
angels, devils,
cherubs and little demons:
there is no one there to say them nay.

Only on this wondrous earth does God reside.
Only in man's body and his priceless brain
does He hold Court;
and only He
can make a heaven or hell of this unbegotten paradise:
where earth and water nudge mankind—
and God is everywhere.

Again
For Bobby

Again—
again the wild harvest—
again the bitter weeds of pain—
again the gun,
the bullets,
and the life of a man hangs trembling in the balance
before the cord is cut
and the life dies out:
again the foul seed, full blown—
again this age hovers on destruction:
again
again
we reap the wild onions of our choosing:
again we shrug,
mindless:
again the jungles of hate blow over us
and we gather in
the melancholy harvest of our sins.

A pocket full of sadness

Once upon a midnight,
clearly on a night the Christians hold so dearly,
and lovely to behold,
the world lay stark and cold and dreary.
Deeply had the nations pondered,
wondered on the reasons for the cold and ice;
wondered on the promise to the people,
of the promises for the brotherhood of man,
promises made in silent wonder,
witnessed by the gods of every nation,
in every mosque and synogogue,
Christian churches far and wide.
All prayed for: peace on earth and to men good will.
And still the stars came sprinkling down
and the moon rode high and smiled—
a mocking smile,
a smile that clearly held a pocketful of sadness
upon this foolish day on earth—
upon this day when peace went crying,
good will, a jester scrawled upon an atom bomb
before it floated down to earth
and spread the gospel of the holy night
for all the world to see.

Autopsy

Where a felon dies,
let him lie.
Let him lie among the outcroppings of shame.
Let him be covered by the morning mists,
yesterday's papers.
Let there be no hue and cry,
no gloating over death.
Only a felon has died:
hands which knew no law,
eyes which saw no sun
and never hailed a star to climb aboard.
Let him vanish—
as the rains which beat the trembling earth
to clothe it in glory—rainbow-hued;
as the winds
which wash our righteous sins away.
Let him be dust and sand
and a tiny seed
blown in the wilderness
and lost.

Monastery on a hill

The deep valley lies covered in morning fog—
like a shroud of death
on the naked body on the hill.
The hill itself is bathed in the new sun
which splatters the naked cobbles,
pours into gaping holes,
and through the open windows.
This skeleton refuses to die:
too much of God has entered here—
too many prayers sleep festooned on the walls—
too many years, undisturbed:
too many monks have given up their manhood here
to pray in stony cells
and labor in the green vineyards below.
The grapes remained,
living in wild profusion, uncouth,
entwined around hoary trees,
on scrambled stones
and lying on the lapping waters of the lake
as bathers in an endless siesta—
dreaming;
dreaming perhaps of a better world still to come,
with happier shepherds to cut and squeeze
and age to near perfection
this wonderful living wine.

The two-legged child

Into the sunshine bristling with light,
the two-legged child romps deep in delight.

The earth and the sky are mated as one,
and the child will linger as long as the sun.

Into the shadows deeper than night,
the two-legged child will wander in fright.

Into a cavern when daylight is done,
the two-legged child sleeps long without sun:

long without sunlight,
long without sky,
the cavern will hold him
till Time will die.

Mon Ami

The tide of burial waits not for man.
The tide comes in
plucking the rootless driftwood on the beach
and floating it away upon a sea of blackness
never to return,
while riding lightly on the laden tide—
amœbas—
tiny little things of minus moment.
The driftwood bobbles aimlessly about,
amœbas in—driftwood out.
No hail—*auf wiedersehn*—
a silent passing in the silent night
when old life ebbs and new life is begun:
and for Joseph Auslander
adrift somewhere in his greatest poem—
farewell.

Codicil for a wayward poet

Once upon a furious lifetime—
once upon an age when the rivers ran dry
but the earth ran red,
where the beat of the sun wrinkled the face of
the earth
and made it brown and hard
and yielding only of its bitter crops—

Once upon a lifetime, a child was born,
born of the bitter feuds and bitter harvest,
born also of the bitter winds which blossomed
over Europe
and blew the vagrant seeds on alien shores.

A poet could hardly wish for more
than to be born in a land where every neighbor
is alien to man,
where every street is a piece of no-man's soil
and guarded like a fortress under siege.

Born one inconsequential day,
one scratch child,
parents
inconsequential,
religion
minor—not desirable,
the child,
small, scrawny,
with lips that sang.

The people wondered
how an asp could sing,
make poems out of clay—
and why they were elated and disturbed.

The monstrous years rolled by.
The dying died.
New rulers came and went.
The Kaisers returned to the earth;
the Hitlers, too.
The little men of Russia came forth to rule
and they, too, came and went:
and even the Chinese coolie was a lord
and gloated in his hideous mask—
all in the name of Brotherhood and the late
Karl Marx.

The poems fell on idle winds,
were buried in the snowdrifts of the Alps,
the rivers of the Jordan,
the fields of France and Burgundy;
and peace, when it came, was a farce.
The rich were surely richer,
the poor, still poor,
and the dead were very dead and far beyond
remembering.

The new day was a day of science and exultation:
"to the moon—
to the stars"—
everything was up and up,
only Peace was down,
understanding, down,
Brotherhood—
a silly poet's dream,
a nightmare floating on atomed winds.

The poet sang, wrote,
and his words drifted into the clay ears
of the multitude,
who did not hear.
The songs fell upon the desert,
but no flowers bloomed.
No substance grew.
The waters froze in the oceans.
The fishes died,
the small—the large
the hunters and the hunted
the good and the evil
the wise and the fools—
all died.
Even the poet died
and his song ended.
A voice unheard in life
should surely be still in death.
His will was buried with his breath
and covered with the ashes.

Now this codicil:
a codicil for a dead poet
alive in his grave—
in his books—his songs;
alive perhaps on some other day
in some other boy
with a happier song
for living ears.

The inner ring

In the far corner,
in the white tunic of the champ,
blazing with dazzling light—
God.
He stands alone—
without handler or second—
breathing fire:
the champ of all time,
all space.
There is lightning in his fist,
death in each beckoning finger.
The champ is ready.

So many times has the devil died,
the earth cannot contain him.
Yet there he stands in the inner ring
waiting for the bell.
To the howling multitude he is small,
fearful, uncouth,
unable to look the champion in the eye,
minus a tail,
minus horns.
A shout goes up,
"God, it's not the devil standing there,
it's man."

And suddenly,
deep within the well of the wilting earth,
the sound of the opening bell of doom.
God turns,
gazes upon the withered ape.
The stars tumble out of the melting heavens.
There is a clap of thunder,
and again the final gong reverberates
deep and hellish and unconcerned.

The devil has died again.

Words

Out of the living void came sounds—
then words—guttural, short,
simple as the weeds which blossomed in the vales.
Then hallowed by uncounted time—
torrents of words,
words full of wonder and surprise,
words living like trees and flowers,
like the mountains rising to the sun,
like silver flushed from a mine
or diamonds sparkling in rain;
words for man to live by,
words to grow upon,
fantastic words to smother the clawing beasts,
and make us rich, infinite, and whole.

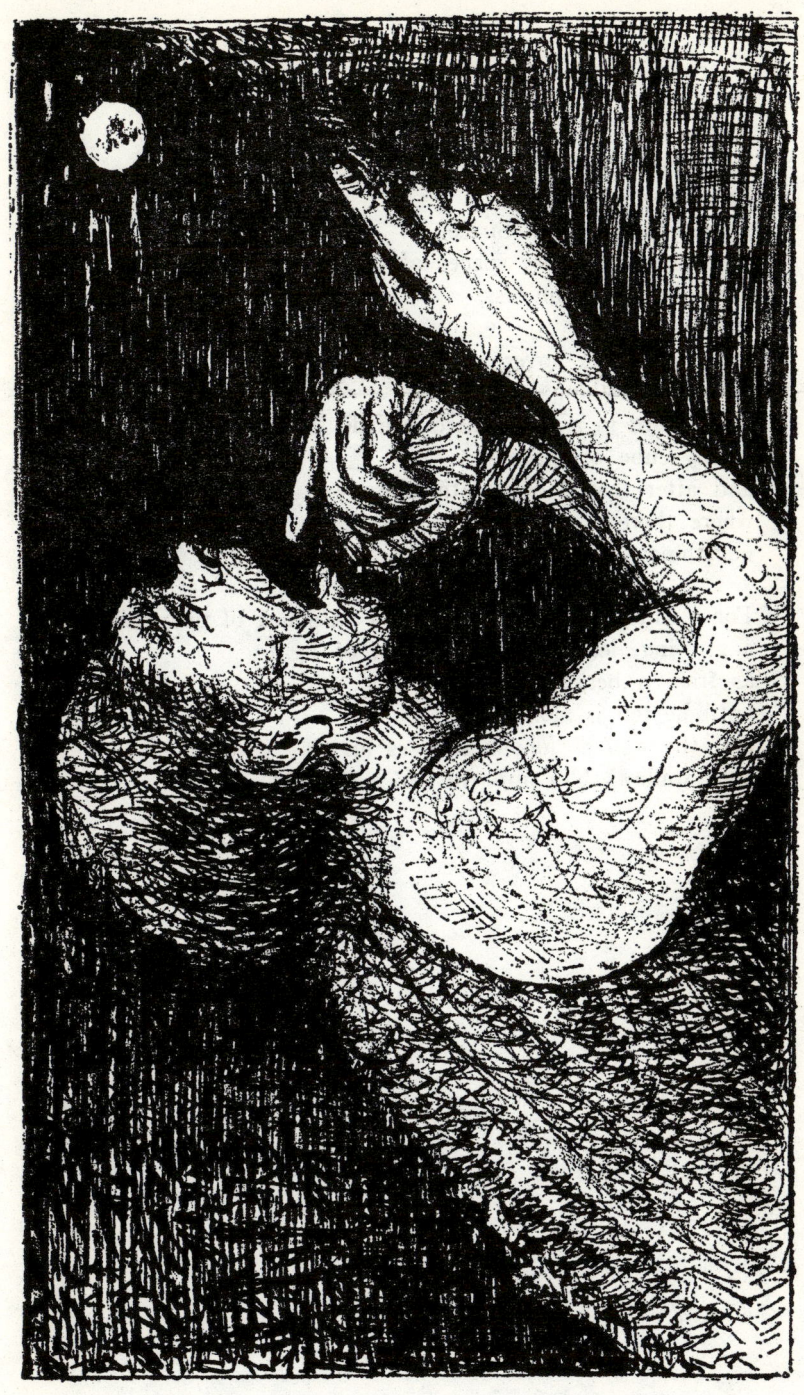

The well of loneliness

Alone—
somewhere—where?
Loneliness is Time
groping and lost in Space.
It covers the empty spaces of Creation.
Time must be timeless,
standing still
while eternities hover all about
and have nothing to say.
For a bird in a cage, there is little time,
a tiny cube of space
and after that a deep fathomless well
where there is neither time nor space
nor things—nor any other bird.

For a child in his crib, there is a yardstick of time and space,
a growing, learning, pouring out of light
as from a benediction
until he too is alone—
and the well of loneliness rises up
and swallows him into the voiceless void.

Poetry night

Mediocrities,
tired,
old,
overdressed,
overfed,
gentle of speech and demeanor
(even the stupid candidates hoping to spear a vote),
their small eyes peering into a blurred tomorrow.
Soon the gay-starched beetles will speak—
a Rabbi, a Mayor, a Judge, a Priest—
but who will speak for poetry?
Who will speak for dead songs falling from dry branches,
dead minds trampling over green earth,
crushing the living flowers, the simple grasses
and every tiny crawling thing below,
unseen,
unheard,
unmissed.

Breathe easy, boy

The sky is very young today,
the trees exceeding green,
and the grasses tall and fresh
for little feet to trample on:
for little minds to wander and explore this massive Universe;
these stubborn hills to conquer,
a sentinel tree to climb upon,
to be a sailor searching out
a strange mysterious isle.

The sky is very young tonight,
and a breathless boy sleeps,
overwhelmed,
flushed,
breathing hard and fast,
sweating,
his empire lost in **dubious fog**
but floating ghost-like all around.

Breathe easy, boy.
A boy has many days
and wondrous nights,
a million worlds to feast upon,
a time to grasp and hold—
but only a single night to sleep.

Wherein the leopard eats his skin

Crazy leopard,
go into the forest for your meal.
Here in the so-called gentle places on this earth
no honest leopard can survive.

Silly leopard,
your teeth and fangs are minor things;
your claws, a baby's rattle.
We have a Universal Law, leopard,
which says
that only if you labor shall you eat:
and whoever heard of a leopard in Detroit,
or even Pittsburgh or New York.
We have such things, silly leopard,
you could never understand,
things to murder every leopard everywhere
and all the other beasts he feeds upon.

Better yet—
come out of the forest, leopard—
go find yourself a museum,
fill out a card,
grovel in a corner
among the debris of ancient things,
and sleep the ages through.

Mi-lady

Steeped in the garb of domestic tranquility,
the garments hung on her like the bodice on a knight.
The battle axe was a broom,
the enemy,
visible and invisible,
hemmed her in.
This was a war unto death.
Behind her, artillery;
two pails mixed with deadly mortars.
They could have been bowmen,
their arrows shining in the sun,
or spearmen hidden in a nearby forest
waiting for the bugle call.
She stood there, proud, anxious,
estimating the time and place for the charge,
the losses which the field of honor would cover,
the final victory
when the field would be sweet and clean
and lovely to behold:
as any house made ready for Christmas day.

Into the night

Into the night, with soft voices drowning
the bitter memories of the icicles of day:
into the night,
obliterating chaos,
confusion in the ant hills,
and in the steeples where old men hide
from the garish suns their own iniquities have conjured up:
into the night, the voices of ignorance seem softer,
the voices of reason, reasonable,
melting the icicles holding our famished feet in bondage,
freeing our fingers,
opening our eyes to the light of billions of stars
and a full yellow moon to see by,
ears to listen to the symphonies of night—
full blended,
leaving the poet wondering:
if this be darkest night,
what joys the morning sun could bring?

Vespers at high noon

Keep the faith, baby,
keep the faith.
Throw the bottle, baby,
burn.
Destroy your neighbors' houses
and his stores.
Steal his goods.
Burn them, baby,
burn.

Kill, baby, kill.
Keep the wild orgies flowing.
Fire the lovely shotgun, baby.
Watch it kill:
and if your sight survives the ashes,
look around you, baby,
look.
Your world is strewn to bits about you,
like shards and ashes from the ladders of your dreams:
and you can simper like a whining jackal,
baby,
without a single faith to keep.

How to catch a metaphor

Pin him down—
the elusive little bastard.
But how?
He flits around in my thumping head
like a mocking mosquito,
just far enough away
to taunt me with a swat
and buzzingly flits away.

It's a stupid game.
"Come on, Joe,
you catch me."

I lie down on soft grasses,
look up to pink and purple ether,
white sailing detergent in the skies,
green apartments in the trees for domestic tranquility,
a baby breeze headed home—
and all around me
the vesper songs of Nature fill my ears.

And while I listen in wonder and in awe,
a sharp chop into an unprotected ear
and the metaphor arrived.
But the bloody bringer of the poet's wine,
I murdered for his trouble and his need.

Cry the innocents abroad

Abroad—
abroad in the vast waste lands of this land,
the innocents cry in their hunger.
The black man hungers to be white.
Daub the black man white.
Turn loose the spray kettles on the multitudes of black.
Daub them white.
Daub them white man also white—
wholesale.

Daub the shacks white,
the palaces white.
Bleed the spray cans until the wind is gone,
all the paint is gone
and the whole stinking mess of black and white,
slave and master,
home and hovel,
disappear—
and all will be lily white,
pure,
insipid,
dead.
And no cry will go up from the land.
Courts and Congresses will disappear,
and only the sad billboard of white on white
will remain
to teach one errant child the simple truth
that not with paint alone will man survive.

An open letter to Yevtushenko

Dear poet:
(and I must confess that poetry is as dear to me
as it is to you.)
I was deeply moved by your tolerance,
your understanding of the Spirit of evil
and your striking out against the animals
who drained the soil of Babiy Yar with blood.
You made the Jews your brothers—
and you wept for them—
as a latter-day Pushkin, you wept,
eloquently,
as only a Russian poet can weep.
It is also true, my friend,
our washing machines cannot erase the blood of our Kennedys,
our King,
and certainly not our Lincoln,
whom you much admire.
But ponder, fellow poet:
each depravity was that of a single beast.
We have no Babiy Yars in America—
no Czecho-Slovakias.
I do not mean to say we live as angels.
We have our injustices—
our cross to bear in Viet Nam.
Our people cry out
and we shall uproot the primitive minds who spawn them
and cast them into oblivion.

Weep then, my friend,
weep for us for Viet Nam.
Weep also for Czecho-Slovakia,
and for all the tiny helpless peoples
the despots overwhelm.

Prophesy

Old Isaiah,
screwing up one jaundiced eye,
taking a long sniff at the pollenized atmosphere
and a longer slide into the heart of memory,
observing the clouds maneuvering before the sun,
and knowing his reputation stood at the post of execution,
closes both his eyes,
dilates his nostrils,
sucks in his breath,
then slowly as the Spirits beckon,
on wings of an unrepentant wish,
he soars and dreams;
until finally reaching the land where Nirvana reigns,
with nothings and nothings everywhere
and breathing in the light of understanding
and finding that nothing is the absolute everything of all,
he slowly opens first one eye,
then the other,
unwraps the wrinkles from his brow,
breathes deeply of the solid air of earth,
and then with circumstance bereft of pomp,
he murmurs;
"It will rain tonight."

Next stop—heaven

Somewhere in heaven
I stepped off a gliding rainbow
marked "ten millionth floor—
hosiery, draperies,
ladies wear,
notions."
And I had a notion, too.
Could this be heaven
where the angels sing *(en masse)*
eternally
or has this damned heavenly escalator been subverted by the devil,
its needle jammed
and going forward
backwards into Hell
and the drear old earth economy?
For heavenly bodies,
I saw salesladies with wings,
floorwalkers sporting haloes,
the store dick without a stick—
and no raspy registers
to toll the knell of parting pay.

The preacher never told me.
His prexies didn't know.
Only I
watching the shining floors go up and up
into the hollow blue
until my eyes saw nothing—blue
and all the ridiculous notions disappeared
into a dazzling world, ethereal blue,
wherein the blanket air was blue,
the voices blue, transparent,
and dancing like a sunbeam
after rain.

Let joy be unconcerned

This is not the age to gather in the lilies
or strew the byways with accolades and song.
We all get educated in the mass,
string out like marchers on the Fourth.
We all can read
and write,
decipher blue prints,
hold a job,
and dig a somewhat nook to hide in
until the magic age when S. S. comes along.
With joy we leave the tired old woodwork,
perambulate a trailer
or a modest place
where the southern sun beats warmish all the year
and vegetate
until we die.
Oh, yes,
we raised a brood of sturdy saplings,
married them,
helped them to mature,
welded them to a job,
a desk to wear
and do their daily stints according to the book.
"My country 'tis of thee"
we sing.
Let joy be unconcerned.

Somewhere

Out there, somewhere, where vastness is a puny word
defined by Science as simply Space
and by man, addicted to a God, as Heaven—
out there, space is a bluish void,
infinite, beyond measure,
empty of life and sound or even meaning
so that the mind of man is lost in contemplation and confusion,
and the labyrinth of his thinking floats outwardly in the void,
then back to earth
as baffling enigmas piled on fathomless inponderables.
But always the mind gropes within the blackness of the puzzle.
Always the Don Quixotes cast their quivering lances upon a moon-
       less star
as if the silent rolling hunk of stone possessed celestial music man
       could make his own:
and the strike, when it came, would prove that every floating star
       was merely a floating windmill,
that every silly lance, a wooden spear,
nebulous,
disposable,
childish,
along with other childish myths.
His reason tells him the heavens will tell him nothing,
nothing of God or man
or why the orbits roll and spin
(like children's tops);
and man will dream and wonder--
how far—how long—how deep—
how infinite is infinity:
and for whom?

Johnny Appleseed

A fool he was,
sleeping with the pigs at night,
his bag of seed a pillow,
and his blanket, a dream:
a dream that the dreary miles he trudged
would some day turn him back to home—
home and haven in the snug little village of his birth,
and that the dreary farms about
would grow delicious apples—
fruit of the gods,
and life for man.
And everywhere he trudged
orchards grew,
but the dogs still whittled at his heels,
the stupid still laughed,
and Johnny still slept with the pigs
and trudged his miles until he died.

A century is like a day.
The trees still blossom white in the spring
and in the fall, the harvest baskets still rest golden in the barns.

Today I passed a marker where he lived,
a seeming symbol of a dead philosophy
no longer pervading the mind of man.
Before me,
a river of stone rolled on
in endless undulations
crossing and recrossing
where once a lonely fool had passed
and planted seeds for his fellow men,
seeds of love and hope,
apples
all tied together in one brotherhood of understanding:

Johnny the god—the man
who slept beside the pigs
and planted seeds
for a fulsome harvest still to come.

Fishing expedition

It's a ponderous rolling restless ocean,
pimpled by tiny island dots
dozing on a pompous bay,
with tongues of sand sticking out, defying the grasping waters
and holding back the alien seas.
Beyond my little spit of land,
beneath,
in floating cities, each separate race
meanders aimlessly about
in perpetual motion—
without calendar, gods, or laws.

Yea—but they live by the Law,
cherish it
and perish by its inexorable Commandments:
"eat and be eaten—
increase and multiply
and ye shall inherit the seas
and the riches thereof.
Beware thou only of the waterless air
and the breed of men who dwell thereon."

It happened.
I bobbled along like a speck of common weed
on a gentle heaving playful ocean,
casting a slender line baited with a sliver of my decimated cousin.
I understood the Law,
salaamed the deity in his infinite wisdom
and settled back
awaiting the greedy mouth to strike
and taste for himself the steel morsel
which cunning man alone contrived.

It's a ponderous yawning ocean.
The sun, playing on its lithe blue muscles,
rippled like a boxer flexing his finger tips.
It's a deceitful vicious ocean,
full of hidden traps to take my matchstick shelter
and scatter the pieces to the straining winds
and cast me headlong, along with my baited cousin,
into the hungry mouths impatiently waiting.

The tired sun sank redly in the west,
the breezes stirred the ocean into foam.
I pulled my useless cousin up,
threw him back into the angry ocean,
and headed back for land.

Hart Crane

Boozer,
brawler,
boisternick,
all of his own choosing and design,
poet—
Searching for some abstract pinnacle of truth,
some piece of beauty hidden in a howling slum
or the curvature of a maddening breast.
Life was a horrible scramble of the elements
pounding into his ears
and blinding him with its ugliness and its light
or revealing the brutality of its wisdom.
And he, Hart, was breasting it,
the entire whirlpool of living from which there was no escape—
except of course by dying;
dying quickly in the deep grey green of a limitless ocean
which offered peace, order,
and the everlasting time to forget.

Vengeance is mine

And why?
and why must the Lord reap the whirwinds of Creation
and why on Him alone?
Vengeance is the twist on a tiny mind
which twirls on sanity
or fumbles into chaos
and is confused with Right and Justice
or simply greed.
Vengeance is a poisoned arrow in the heart
or poisoned clouds
when all horizons have been stilled.
Why must the Lord be burdened with the load,
on whom the thunderbolt—
His kith,
His kin—
cast in His own image?

Only the wind remembers

Only the wind remembers,
remembers in his race across the skies,
to return to man,
to blow across his fields and bring him rain,
to howl across empty wastes with undiluted fury,
as any buccaneer
bearing down upon a helpless hacienda
to strip it clean,
to pull down great ships, steel bridges,
and the teeming ant hills mankind assembles
and calls it home.
The wind has a seeing eye, a twisted brain,
and an empty heart.
Yet only the wind remembers
that he is Lord and Master here;
that puny man
must bend and tremble before his anger or his whim,
or weep for joy when a gentle breeze
brings home the Springtime once again.

Wiggly
(The wench from Piggly Street)

On my block
most anything goes.
On the corner lot—Guziewkowitz;
Joe the barber, to you.
Next door—old Sally,
the widow woman;
her man now ten years gone:
but not old Sally,
alive and kicking.
It was fun to watch her wiggle up the street.
The walk is straight,
correctly engineered,
smooth and even;
but not for Sally
on her short, fat, dumpy legs
bowed out a little.
She ran in arcs,
rhythmed—semi-right, semi-left,
and forward just a little.
Sally cooked for uncle Pete;
chief cook and bottle washer,
waitress, maid, and clean-up girl.
She was the crew.
The truckers loved to kid her every time
and say if they were rolling down the Pike
like Sally,
the cops would pin a "driving while"
on each of them
and haul them off to jail.

The day old Sally failed to come,
Peter swore and growled.
At nine, on closing time,

he called on Sally, with fire in his eye.
He saw the sad old run-down clock
was still.
The wiggly body, cold, serene,
and laid out straight without a curve
or arc:
a thing of many sadness,
on our block.

Then I was merely a boy

It is always morning for a boy.
All the small clouds have disappeared.
The wind has puffed itself home to rest
somewhere in the wild beyond
and much too far away for a boyish head to wonder about.
The sun is up,
warm, alive,
pressing on his neck, his arms,
hiding in his hair
and laying a mask of life over his eager face,
putting ginger in his feet—
to walk—to run—to fly—
ginger in his eyes
to make them sparkle in the light
to catch the rainbow as it dips to earth
and ride the wild spectrum to its lair.

But then I was merely a boy.

The kiss is on the rose

What makes the morning shine so clear
and sprinkles dew upon the grass?
What makes the scented breezes kiss
an upturned budding rose?
There is an alchemy of smell,
of sight and hope and feeling;
a welding of the sky and earth
that brings to June that total joy—
a kiss upon a rose.

And the world spins on

How can you answer a fool—
except by something still more foolish—
a clown,
except with wilder clowning?
And why—
and why must every fool be answered,
every clown applauded
and the whole tumult of life reduced to fools and clowns,
while the world spins on?
The eons come and go,
unperturbed,
as if the fools and clowns were sand upon a worthless beach.
The waves roll over them,
and in time the fool and his questions are buried,
the clown and his clowning,
(like a shell swept into the gathering ocean),
lost—
while the world spins on—
unconcerned.

Why should I weep?

Why should I weep and wring my bleeding hands?
Why should my spirit shrink when uncouth feet
Have desecrated all my father's lands
And left their heritage for me to meet?
Why should I look to heaven and pray—or hate
The dismal world the naked dawn revealed?
Why should I weep for this my lost estate
When I, roughshod, destroy my brother's field?
We think of Justice with an ego mind:
Our little rights are dearly husbanded,
And each with bitter sanctions is entwined
To break the weary trespasser instead.

Oh, I should weep—but I laugh to think
To what devilish humor the world can sink.

The bouquet woman

Old and bent—
like the hickories of her native Indiana,
with an antique marbleized face
and gnarled fingers,
she stood there by her easel—
and I watched her barren land begin to bloom with flaming brush
        strokes,
trees and rivers,
old remembered houses,
waters,
mountain tops:
but always the flowers.
She made her vases squat and ugly
but breathed her life into the flowers.
She saw the worlds of yesterday
idealized by time
and made them into mountain sides.
She saw the restless driven oceans,
but her happy thoughts
she fashioned into flowers and trees
even trees that were dead or old,
gnarled like her fingers,
spread themselves like living fauna across her canvas world:
and I thought—
Did it really matter if she were not a Picasso?

Oddly he dies

Men have always died
and always will.
Born in useless pain,
he lives in pain,
(a gift, no doubt, of Nature to keep the stock alive),
a wooden horse to lull him to tranquility
before the final twit which welds him into clay and earth.

But not today.
Except for wars, massacres, murders,
atomic poisons,
and the miracle of industrial dregs,
man lives—
a hypochondriac to the killer of pain,
worshipping the Great God Aspirin,
the opiates
and the dull trash of entertainment
until his day is done.
And the sorry child,
the mouse caught in a revolving trap,
races breathlessly
painlessly,
and stupidly
to death.

Manic depressive

I—
I am the center of all eyes,
staring, gloating,
and pointing their obscene eyeballs at me.
I can see through them:
evil is in their minds,
evil in their hands.
They would catch me if they could,
wheedle me into letting down my guard.
But I am wise—
I know them.
They cannot hide their evil in white
or speak softly to me.
The evil is in their eyes
and they are blind.
Only I can see.
I am cunning.
I will hide—or run away—
away—
far, far away
from the staring, gloating eyes,
from obscene eyeballs telling me dirty jokes,
where I can see the world—unseen,
hear the world—unheard,
and they can never find me.

The whiskey rebellion

Stripped down to non-essentials,
booze is booze.
It's like a stripper on a stage—
you never really see the thing you're looking for.
The dose is small and amber.
It gurgles down your throat
and soon everything is dancing way inside.
You think, "Another one and I'll be set to go."
You're right, of course; you go.
The room becomes unsteady. You stagger.
Your friends are rolling, too.
"Gotta be an earthquake somewhere":
and then your friend comes past and says,
"Joe, you seem a little rumpled for the night.
Can I take you home?"
And you let him have it—
a sneaky left to his unprotected chin.
That earthquake must be raising havoc someplace.
You lose your balance.
Down you go.
It's safer anyway.
The lights go out
and darkness hides you while the heavens scream
and murky tigers dance around you
heaving bottles at the monkeys in the trees.

It's a long road

It's a long road that has no ending.
It's a very sad ending for those who never trekked.
For a black boy sixty-five years ago
there was no road bending to the sky.
No sky showed through the avalanche of smoke
pouring out of stacks
and into his lungs.
How can you fathom the mystery of creation
which makes one man beggar,
the other king, poet,
which shrinks one man to a lump of sodden clay
and makes the other, god,
creator of songs,
poetry,
sage
and seer?

The black boy lived,
precariously,
wrote his poems, his plays,
spoke his mind on Justice
until the world began to understand
that God can live inside a black skin
as well as white;
that each is brother to the rest:
and for all of that, Langston Hughes,
you have lived and died
and yet remain among the living
as poet, seer, and sage.

Wanted—A Minister of the Interior

Somebody with an outrageous mind,
well trained,
executive, administrator;
somebody who can look me over on the outside
and know me deep within;
someone who can ravel out my moods
and make them simple—
even for me to understand;
someone to take my hand
and make me sizzle with excitement,
with anticipation and with hope;
someone I can marry and call him Love;
someone to help me bear my children
and be a father,
even as he husbands me
and makes me whole—
as woman, mother, wife:
and for all that his salary will be love and devotion
till I die.

All the world's a stage
and all the people in it, merely players?

Not so, dear William.
The play's the thing, you know,
but to actors only,
parrots geared to make-believe,
a clown one day,
a king the next,
and every day a fool but Sunday.
It's much too bad, O worthy one,
you spent your time in courts and theatres
where artifice is king,
deception, queen,
and the common herd, the noisome in-between.
You sang of kings and lords,
princesses,
merchants, jesters, and the like,
but not a single play, dear William,
and hardly ever a cadenced line
of that stout breed of Englishmen
who wrested "Merrie England"
from the gaudy gentry of your day.

Time is a dragon

Time is a dragon with hellish claws,
with pits of fire belching from its soulless belly.
The dragon always gets you in the end
and you go—down into that bottomless pit
and disappear,
taking nothing with you,
leaving nothing behind,
the ashes of your memory blown and scattered by empty winds,
as seeds from a pod,
finding perhaps a new piece of scratch soil to rest upon
while Time,
like a gypsy eel,
glides quietly along,
unperturbed.

During the night

During the night the arch of Archemides
lifted a fragile planet to the skies
and sent it hurtling into space,
there to roam in orbit with other hunks of stone
pulled by the great demon Sun
and pushed by lesser demons
until the sweating earth lay mired in muck and water
and rolled like a giant crooked mud-ball in the sky.

During the morning when the Lord and Archemides got together
to view their daily handiworks,
The Lord groaned.
"Archemides, my son,
I have made you Lord of mathematics and science.
For everything, excepting me, of course,
(and here the Lord grinned a little)
there is rule and reason.
With my fulcrum you have pushed a world,
lifted it out of nowhere,
set it in motion,
a world of mud and stone and water.
I will help you, Archemides.
In the fulness of time, I will create life,
and very much later, Archemides, you will be born.
You will live through many days and many nights—
and you will learn.
Also you will teach the sciences to man—
man not yet begot:
and in the end you will die.
You will learn that life and death will spin themselves into eternity,
even as the earth and planets spin,
rolling into nothing where there is neither time nor space.
A speck of my grand design you will study
and pass your knowledge on to other men

until they, too, may one day come to know
that God and man are really one,
indefinable,
inseparable:
that every living creature is a god,
and God, a living creature:
that every brackish clod is also God—
and I, God,
the meanest little clod."

The Lord sighed.
Archemides scratched his furry head:
and so it came to pass.

Corridor of dreams

I'm in a little room,
harsh,
ungainly,
scientific,
a sort of penance for a life ill spent.
In the morning—the High Priest.
Later, some lower priests, nuns, helpers, learners,
stethoscopes by the dozen,
needles,
thermometers fore and aft,
pills—wholesale.
I am washed and scrubbed,
sterilized,
catheterized,
panned,
lifted onto a comfortless bed
and served impossible meals.
The High Priest checks my chart,
pats my back—
and the answer—
"Reprieved for still another day."

So much for me.
I'm happy to be alive,
to have some books, writing paper, and peace.
Beyond my door
a long, bright, disturbing corridor,
soft tiling on the floor,
soft shoes treading up and down,
soft talk,
and sometimes, when you least expect it,
a gay, muffled, but hilarious piece of laughter.
This is the river of life,

pulsating with energy,
moving on and out.
Here, in the shadows, we wait
(like in any dockyard)
to have our sails repaired,
the bulkheads welded;
and if the craft is done for sailing,
has seen her last horizon disappear
where the gypsy green melds with the blue eternal sky:
and suddenly the sun is in your face
while the ship sinks quietly into the abyss of forgotten things
and disappears.

Lecture from my hospital bed
(For Sister Josephine, nurse)

"You know you break the bond for all eternity.
No man will ever call you wife—
no children, mother—
and every one of us you lay a soothing hand upon
will be a stranger,
stranger than the tiny specks of light we call the stars—
each one indifferent to the rest."

As if she read my ailing thoughts,
she smiled
and slipped quietly away.

Menchen—menchen

Drive anywhere,
fly,
take a streetcar, elevator, bus,
take an oxcart, horse, or mule,
or a sad-faced jackass on a Mexican plain.
Take anything,
anywhere.
Behold!
threshed like summer wheat
the grain falls before the reaper of the golden horde.
In Asia, Africa, Europe,
down.
Strewn among the furrowed blistered fields
lie the charred husks of garnered wheat;
a weeping wilderness of open mouths
stilled—forgotten:
transmuted by a monstrous alchemy
into gold and trade.

Menchen—menchen
licht darf mir benchen:

have done with war
treaties, arms,
bombs:
have done—
have done.

Angels Paradise

There is a time when angels love to sing,
when every tree and shrub is music to their ears,
a time to hang their halos on a limb,
and like weary humans
lie down upon the sun-drenched fields,
or beneath a green umbrellad tree,
and dream:
to dream of children romping on the lawns,
old farmers drying corn,
apples dangling from the laden trees
with a spot of rosy red, just ripe for eating:
so dreaming—to become a human child again,
untroubled,
as if the tempting apple still lingered on the tree.

With both my hands
(For George Grill)

My heart is as this stone,
with you, but very much alone.
The mind would be consoled.
Since death must gather in its fold,
myself, as well as you,
I cannot hold it but as true
that time unites these hands much more
than your dear breath before.

New wine for old

The wine glass drips the sparkling liquid
back into the sorry sod
to lie among the shards of other useless things;
old bones—unwanted,
old stones, once seething in their infancy
and now quite obdurate, congealed,
old crawling flesh
undone by Time
and seeking metamorphosis with other flesh
to be reborn,
refurbished,
and laugh at Time's unhumored stance
with the wild debris around it.

Only the wine drips slowly down.
The brittle glass stands firm,
mirrored in the raging sun,
changeless,
more obdurate than stone
and waiting for the season's harvest press
to squeeze new wine
for the shining glass to spill.

Man—supergod

God—
rootless,
fruitless,
barren of human emotions;
without Spirit
or design;
God being merely God.

Down in a tiny hollow,
too far away for notice,
too small,
insignificant
and dull,
God's effigies skulk among the outcroppings of **earth,**
crawling over the wastes,
burrowing,
rising above the clouds
to see and wonder at the Divine alchemy
and to reason quite abstrusely
that all this wonderful chemistry,
these laws and bounties,
were made for him alone.

After all—
who else could glorify murder
wholesale
and call on God for reference
to underwrite his crimes?

Manhattan skyline

Buildings sleep in the evening
like empty beehives on a mountain top
steeped in deep repose.
And all the time,
watched over by crawling moon-silver
and the garish lights below,
they stand alone,
tall,
gaunt,
silent,
ungainly,
framed in somber darkness,
ruminating,
their twinkling eyelids slowly closing
one by one
until the naked giants
sleep—
like grotesque demons in the sky.

Farewell to farms

A long disgusting farewell to the conglomeration of junk strewn
    aimlessly about,
the old mansion house standing stupidly on one foot
and being held up by forty layers of paper on the walls,
the stinking outhouse,
the barn, the woodshed, the pigpens,
the rusty implements rotting in the summer weeds.

Yet here I am,
Lord of all I survey,
the stony acres,
the indifferent crops,
the sulphur drinking water
and a wife with sense enough to keep the peace.
The boys have driven off to fatter pastures,
the girls, married and raising multitudinous broods—
which leaves us nothing but a longing to be free,
to say farewell—
to sell the whole lousy kit and kaboodle,
except the flivver
and go:
God willing—
anywhere.

"Wherein doth lie the dread and fear of kings"

Fear roots on a stricken tree,
gnarled and dead,
barren
except for the cowering vulture above
where the topmost branch is home.
From there the sky feasts down upon the earth,
the earth drinks in the sky:
and even when the lovers quarrel, they are one,
inseparable
until Time itself shall cease to crawl into eternity
and run away and hide.

Fear lives in the heart of every man,
crowds his brain into an empty gunny sack,
his courage leaving him
as Life itself when a hybrid dream departs.

Fear eats into the savage fingers of the artist
splotching his work, his mind,
until he melds like a vulture to the scaffold tree
and picks his rotted flesh and bones
to assuage his grief.

Old Bowery

Perhaps you've never even looked for romance there;
Perhaps an unknown fear comes over you;
The dirty uninviting streets—faces
Sallow, sullen in the sickly lamplight,
Grimacing, scowling, as you pass them by,
Intensely burning eyes which seek and peer,
And hands, untrained, famished, and unrestrained.

Above, a screeching, grinding monster rolls
Out of the murk of rails and sentry lights,
Plowing the darkness on slender greenish
Endless ribbons of steel, past aged piles
Of brick, four stories high, wherein by grace
Of some petty theft, beggary, or toil
The lowest humans ease their earthly woes
For some brief hours, and change their thankless lot
From an uncomprehending dreamless day
To the sotted heaven of a drunken sleep.

Morning stroll

This aged pen of mine,
Steeped in the bright red ink of fire,
The black of death,
The green of clutching avarice,
The purple of confusion and of lust,
Dips queerly in the soft white liquid of the early dawn.
The paper scratches,
But still no words come forth upon the waiting canvas.
No structure rises,
No trees nor shrubs,
Nor the curious little figures in the human mold
To disport themselves
And whisper tales
For the mind to feast upon
And the eyes to see.

The time is not for words nor paint nor brush.
The naked canvas, like the naked day,
Is nothing
Until the paint of time shall weave its destiny
In the motley colors of the day and age,
And I, perhaps, shall then make poetry
From the burned-out ashes of the day-old dream.

Save my child

Often, when I was a boy
playing with marbles on a milk-shake street,
or walking to school,
or away from school
(like for instance on a Friday afternoon when I could
look ahead with pleasure to a swell Saturday and Sunday)
to many games of marbles,
or underleg—if I had some pennies—
and just about the time I began to feel good all over,
suddenly the clang, clang of the fire bells—
and off I went after them—
with my thin little legs pounding the pavement:
and finally a great crowd—
all kinds of funny noises,
crazy shouting in six languages
none of which I understood
(being just a Yiddish kid from the East side).
But the fire was real,
the horses grand,
the hoses stretched all over—
and way up on the fifth floor some ladies were hollering.
A fine Irish fireman was climbing a high ladder,
water was swishing to the sky
and making a pink and purple rainbow—
and I don't even know for sure if the child was saved,
but it was fun while it lasted.

Convocation

Strung out like a convoy of Arabs
on a darkening wind-swept plain,
my sparrows come a-calling.
They roost on the wires in endless array
staring at the evening sky
and the foolish man below,
wondering about a supper long delayed;
or perhaps of other things to chirp about—
the vicious little boys with BB guns,
the lack of water,
the torrid sun parching out the grasses
or perhaps their certain instinct which says
    "Summer is going—
     beware—beware."
But there they sit,
motionless,
framed in the deep blue of a summer sky
and the last of the great orange ball
sinking slowly down behind the trees
to rest.
Then just as suddenly they were gone.
The early night rose up and fanned the heat away.
All the tribes of nature spoke their billion pieces,
recorded their complaints
and fell asleep:
and I too watched, waited, and wondered
and finally fell asleep.

Descent and distribution

I am I,
the center of everything around me.
So are the squirrels and acorns
and the baby squirrels who inherit his estate.
Everything that lives and breathes
and recreates its kind
garners his estate and leaves it to his progeny
to have and to hold.
My squirrel died and left a tree
and three impish squirrels after him.
I wouldn't want to quarrel with his title,
but it was his tree—
and all the acorns he could hide were his to eat
or pass them on to the lady squirrel
and the little imps.
He never saw the BB that shot him dead
or the frightful boy who did it,
but the imps (now grown) mourned beside him on the grass
and soon forgot.
Only the tree remained.
The acorns grew
and the imps chattered and were happy with their estate.

The Assyrians came down

By plane and train
and telephone
by car and creaking spar
they yawled and crawled
hid and slid
to Babylon.

The flesh was here
drear and dear
the bones still firm:
the soul of Joseph Auslander,
his hat awry
one eye in wink
the other scorn
gazed down upon the horde
and grinned—
"My books—my rooks—
my manuscripts—
bargain day at Macy's"
and then one further look—
two white-skinned lambs
shuddering—
and the frameless poet shook
convulsed with rage
and fled piteously away.

The crowning

Silver fish or baldy pate,
a crown is still a crown,
a noble sentiment made of tin
or silver,
gold perhaps—
and sometimes, for a life ill spent
in stealing the swelling granaries of this August world,
her treasures, arts,
a priceless crown,
emerald-studded
with diamonds thick as fleas
resting on the smelly carcass of a beast,
who prides himself as man,
a king is crowned,
high priest of a new and noble Order (so called),
older than Methuselah,
bigot, cheat,
murderer—
and therefore fitting to be crowned Monster of the Universe,
Lord of the despoiled peoples under his bilious fingertips,
the very same fingers
which placed the sordid crown
upon his sordid balding pate.

And as Shakespeare said—
"Now wherefore sit ye idling."

Will of the wisp

My mind wanders like a wandering Jew
through cloistered seminaries,
among the hill-tops where the raging winds sweep clean
the accumulated rubbish of mankind
and only the bare stones stand bold and solemn,
like accusing headstones mocking the deceased.

My mind floats like a rubber ball
on the tiniest stream of consciousness
where only a practised eye may see
and a practised heart enjoy.

The ball floats like a crimson bubble,
fragile and bright,
disintegrating at a wisp
and soon forgotten.

My mind is a plaything,
scenario,
book—
a library of books tumbling all about me
while I scramble and reach,
grasping an unsure treasure
and treasure it till I die.

Consequently I'm it

In my youth I played volley ball,
tag,
wolf are you ready,
potsie on the sidewalk,
underleg, when I had three cents or more;
and always there was one guy who was it.
He always lost the games,
and panting, he would sneak away towards home.
There, if he were lucky,
he could steal a nice big hunk of cake from the kitchen
and read and munch,
where hidden away in the fairy land of books, he could always
      be the hero,
win the games,
throw the javelin the furthest,
vanquish his enemy with battle-axe or sword
and carry off the princess, holding her dearly
until the morning bell said,
"up-up-up-up"—and he sleepily turned it off.

In the end you came to know
you never really win the game.
Youth, on its spidery wings,
disappears.
The games are childish
and a man has many things to do,
ream out a place for his stand in life,
a wife to share it,
children to fill in the hollow places,
and a million crazy things to do:
a dreamless world—
no jousts, no castles,
no games,
just sweat and tears

and sometimes a little blood.
Only one thing,
in the treadmill of my life,
I did forget.
When the nights were long and quiet,
the room would fill with a swarm of lit-up things,
and all of them carried signs reading
"love"—and they disappeared,
leaving me still "it,"
chasing my own shadow
with my own dubious tail:

and if you're a friend,
don't even ask me to explain.

How tall

How tall am I,
inches, feet, yards,
meters?
How tall are you,
and by what measure will you be judged?
How tall is the world,
the unclimbable crags?
How shall we measure our lives,
by seconds, minutes, hours,
eons?
How tall is a word,
idea, emotion?
How tall is wealth?
How deep is the kettle of poverty?
How high are the weeds,
ignorance, greed, bestiality?

Everything has a measure and a price,
but man,
changing like a chameleon
from saint to sinner,
from man to beast
and beast to man.
The yard stick is a fraud;
no inch, no foot, no yard,
no meter.
Man stands alone,
unmeasurable,
saint, sinner, chameleon, beast,
but somewhere in the imprisoned recesses of his being
there sleeps a spark,
living in its cocoon, eating its way to light,
and to a fathomless destiny no man can comprehend.

Mamie at the hangin'

Stiff as the bristles on his corncob pipe,
she stood there, tall and thin,
her long black dress touching her toes,
her hair severely black
(as is proper for any widow),
her blazing eyes boring into the burly back of the Sheriff.
The hangman stood patiently by,
contemplating the forever thirteen steps where living ends.
Her eyes froze upon her John tied together like a calf at branding.
The rope was on his neck.
The Sheriff read a paper—
not long—
and the telling thump.
John was dead.
Mamie turned, walked back to her carriage,
and drove furiously away.
The road was long, hard, and rocky,
but Mamie saw none of it,
only the piece of ground, some twenty acres—
scrub they called it—
harsh and dry
and fit for nothing.
Jim and John both claimed it,
lawed over it,
John lost.
Jim died—
and now all three were dead.
It was long evening when Mamie came home
and tended her famished brood.
"Whom to kill?
Didn't God mean this matter to be settled?"
The moon said no.
The stars said no.
The evil ground, alive with monstrous mouths,

shouted, no, no, no—
no, Mamie, no.
Mamie listened and fell asleep.
She was dead in the morning.

Unbend

Unbend the night rivets of the yoke,
unbend the meter of your sleep.
Raise up your eyes to where the light still glows
westward at the rim of sight;
westward where mind and matter merge into one lone solitude of
      grace,
one lone unbending sight
before the curfew of the world rings out
and the long ragged night rings in:
where sleep shall have neither sight nor sound
nor dreams nor seasons—
nor any life,
and the nightmare ashes will inherit the land.

Like bundles of snow

The clouds crawl in like bundles of snow
in wisps and shadows,
like a snowman in the sky:
and some float dark and angry,
sailing under spitting winds
to hurl themselves upon the earth
in phalanxed sheets,
whipping up the lightning and the thunder
for the grand assault.
But sometimes on a summer's day,
like white fleece nudging the heavens
and wrapped in mantles of sun,
they float along as fairy castles in the sky:
but all the while, untamed and free
beyond man's grasp or suzerainty.

The bookends

Naked little hussies
made of lead,
looking sweet and childish
and innocent instead.
No father ever sired you—
no mother ever lay
upon the long green grasses
when you were cast away.
You came to life, a genie,
steaming from a copper pot
into a plaster bedstead.
maidened very hot.

Naked little hussies,
bare of breast and thigh,
seeing only books and books
and people passing by,
hoping for a roving eye,
a hand upon your breast—
that you might be a child of **man**
and not a leaden guest.

Numbskull and gnat

Thick as the sludge in my run-down crankcase—
tiny as the pebble my carburetor holds
which keeps my ancient vehicle rusting in the yard
while I,
super-mechanic,
expert in the art of explaining failures,
expert in shuffling in and out of troubles,
but mostly in,
gaze sadly
at my wayward prisoner
standing so patiently at death's door.
I, numbskull and gnat,
resting in my home-made hammock
tied solidly between two giant oaks
diffuse the perplexing problems
by softly rocking my tender bones,
my famished brain
and ponder the horrible notion
of raising up my ailing bucket,
finding a cob-webbed wrench and screwdriver
and giving my dying mule a bedside lift
on its unhappy journey to oblivion.

The trespasser

With only half an eyelid open,
a child can see beyond the dreams of wisest men;
a void—
so big, intense, friendless, and obscure,
magnificent,
the mind of man dazzles to stupidity,
unravels his aching brain like an endless string
gathering in the void to make it finite;
then on to fathom still another void
beyond the stars,
constellations;
with beings perhaps,
non-beings—
until the mind itself grows void
hanging like a coattail on to nothing:
that is nothing but infinity
twinkling from the eye of a child.

Forever eighteen

Gone:
gone into the thin air of seedless memory,
the grey of half-forgotten foolish things
and the deep blue of the fathomless sea:
forgotten and lost.

The eighteen eyes are sparkling blue,
leaping from sound to sight,
from home to school to friends,
parties,
work—
(the drudge is lightly thought);
and even if the silent wheels turn inward—
seventeen, sixteen, twelve,
eleven—
and the turgid waters turn blue,
then black:
"The baby must have died—
the girl mislaid."

And now—
eighteen,
eager,
fresh,
trembling to unfold a wing.

"Look up—up,"
the tutor scolds,
"down is where the ground is."
Up—forever up.
Up where the wide blue sky will open up,
where a girl may float among the floating heather;
up where the clouds no longer roam,
where only the blue of the forever swims
in a total bluish sea

eternally
and where the count forever stands,
eighteen.

Like Gaul

Christendom is divided into three disjointed parts:

INFIDELS
for whom Salvation is a dirty word
or meaningless poppycock;

BELIEVERS (THAT IS)
who find the Book like a head stream
in which to bathe;
where the words are cool, comfortable,
rewarding;
where the current is slow and steady,
onward;
where the stream becomes a river—
and beyond;
a place to feel, believe, desire,
but never a place for flesh to mingle with the flesh **and tide of**
       humanity,

to build a house,
gratify desires
or call your fellow Spirits, brother, father, friend—or man.

SCORNERS
men who find the river wet and cold,
shallow, with hidden rocks to cut and bruise;
empty of the gilded promises,
of endless tomorrows,
empty of the suns and moons,
purpose and design;
empty of that final light
around which the moth will flutter through eternity
to bask and bask:
a world of nothing in an empty sky;
a useless journey—
a simple end.

The island of my dreams

As in a dream,
everything I am
or hope to be
comes floating out of space;
and in the little pocket of my eye,
where everything is dark and hidden
and only the deep illumination from within
brings to my prison
the light, the shadows, and the meanings
of what I seek or ought to be.
Here, there is a clarity in depth,
in understanding,
and sometimes in a dazzling vision
which I still remember
when I awake
and listen to the humdrum noises of my day.
I cannot see nor reach the fabulous cord which holds me to my
        dreams,
but, like the tides,
I am pulled to exotic shores
and left there stranded
while I watch with awe
the miraculous pageants floating by.

International harvester

A tiller, a Teller,
an erudite feller,
his fields are bathed in strontium,
his children, in the cellar.

When I was very young indeed

When I was very young indeed
we sang a little ditty
(with great relish)—
like this:
"My father gave me a nickel
to buy a pickle.
I didn't buy a pickle,"
and then it trailed off into a morass of almost words
and almost music.
We laughed a little
because there never was a nickel.
And I was very young indeed
and really didn't miss it.

Somewhere between the two great wars,
like penny peanuts filtering through my fingers,
the stingy years sneaked by,
breathless,
unwilling to stop for one lone passenger
who didn't even own a fare
or know his destination.
The frowsy cars stormed by,
and watching after it,
the red lights glowed warm, desirable,
leaving me behind, whimpering.
It was swish swish, coming in,
grind grind, going out
with jostling people in and out
rushing everywhere,
but here
where the peanut stand stood idly by
waiting

for one lone gentle boy to slip a penny
and let the peanuts dribble through his sorrowful fingers
while the lighted monster
and the scavengers within
rolled roisterously along:
and the empty tracks strung out
like endless strings bending into one—
with one horizon dimly showing:
for I was very young indeed.

We counted seven

At least I learned to multiply:
seven times two equals fourteen—
and if you add my pa and ma,
sixteen in all.
Sixteen hands at the dining table,
sixteen feet below,
sixteen plates and portions three times daily,
and a basket of mouths—all opened wide.
My pa was big,
barrel-chested, heavy,
gruff of voice and always very stern,
except, of course, when company arrived,
of if ma was ailing,
or one of us got sick.
I remember the railroad flat,
four stories up,
the quarter meter for the gas,
the smelly halls,
and by every door, a different smell.
They said the East side was a ghetto;
Jews on Houston street,
Chinamen down below on Pell,
Italians near the Bowery,
not to mention bums:
and further up, the fancy ones,
the ones we never got to meet.
Time is like a run-down clock,
always standing still:
and yet somehow we grew and grew.
The ghettos hung like aged shrouds upon the line
covering the hulks of ship-wrecked hives we called our street.
The cracks were in the schools, the synogogue,
or perhaps the churches,
(in which we never stepped),
the library on Saturday

and once or twice each summer,
a B.M.T. safari to the Island.
Odd how quickly high school graduation came,
and even college flew on painted wings.
How very odd my parents had become,
illiterate, and rather dull.
But I was bright and fresh,
ambitious,
with a ribboned sheepskin and a lettered trade,
and with my eyes burning in the bright glitter of Wall street
where the money lay.
The table shrank and shrank:
brothers gone away,
sisters married,
mother ailing herself to the grave,
father no longer gruff,
but quiet, tired, dejected,
unimpressed with his achievements
or even ours.
We moved away—
way uptown;
good house, good street, high rent.
We kids were making it.
The man we called our father,
almost a stranger—
reading his Jewish paper,
his Temple friends,
his lonely walks in Central park:
and I got to thinking:
"What fools these mortals be."
I mean all seven of us,
all fourteen hands and feet,
all seven of our educated brains
watering a plastic lily
while the withering vine strangled on the desert hearth,
untended
and alone.

A poet is entitled to a nightmare

I have long loved
and long lost
the alchemy of sound and sight and rhythm,
the meaning of a friendly face,
an artless voice
and the serene companionship of minds and bodies
welded into one.
I have lost the art of contemplation,
the sight of mind no other eye can see
and listened to the razzle-dazzle of newly instructed heads
delving like pincers into the depth of the Universe
to drain it dry, like the grey graveyards of an Oklahoma oil field:
and I am counted on as seer,
revered because of age—
as the dying are revered.
I stand lone and silent,
as a tree no longer bearing fruit,
and with hardly any leaf—
and I wait
for the silent axe to fall.

This hollow idiocy we call Science,
innocent of emotion,
devoid of feeling
unhampered by a thirsting after beauty,
is like an army of miniscule ants
taking over the Universe
and devouring it whole.

The harvest

About me lies the fallow gold of the earth.
This autumn's yield is pregnant
With the load of undelivered life,
Waiting for the ancient midwives of the soil
To tear her children from an uncomplaining womb.

This must be a dream.
The face is beautiful and kind:
Large eyes, wistful of her mission,
A belly, bursting with its store
(Promises of tomorrow and of days to come),
Clothed in the brown and russet garments of her hour,
She seemed a symbol of attainment and high hope.
But I was not deceived—I plucked the garments off.
Wondrous mother—swollen with her yield:
She lay there naked to my hungry eye.
But suddenly I saw them—small—so very small they were;
Black biting vermin crawling over her:
Millions of them—sucking her blood,
Piercing her eyes, stinging her face,
Paralyzing her brain—destroying all,
The living and the things which would have lived:
Then slowly as I watched their ravenous sport,
She disappeared into their thirsting maws,
And all was quiet—quiet—deadly still.

Bitter plums

The pangs of birth are beautiful to behold
on a mother plum at her maiden flowering.
A thousand virgin eyes encased in royal hue
suckle from shining morning breasts
and watch the lazy clouds go sailing by.

The holiday is over.
Gossamer tresses float lightly down,
leaving a thousand babies dangling on the boughs
singing and laughing in the summer breeze:
and soon the fat little bellies will grow and grow,
rocked by the soothing wind,
warmed by hilarious suns,
rain drenched, washed, scrubbed,
their bodies round and soft as any bride on her wondrous bridal
      night.

And then one day a vulgar wind whips rude among the branches.
The rain has a cold wet sting—like death.
The sun is sick,
listless,
and dies behind a mountain of banshee clouds.
The sordid wind comes howling for the kill,
tearing the frightened children from her breasts
and heaving them over the mutilated countryside.
The mother tree,
naked,
disheveled,
bleeding from grievous wounds,
weeps uncontrolledly
for her dying children strewn below.

Date Due